A Heap Of Broken Vessels

Copyright © 2006 by Betty Lou McFall-Perkins

Unless otherwise noted, all Scripture quotations are from The Holy Bible, King James Version

All rights reserved. Except for brief quotations in critical review, no part of this book shall be reproduced or transmitted in any form or by any means, electronic, mechanical, magnetic, photographic including photocopying, recording or by any information storage and retrieval system, without prior written permission from:

Betty Lou McFall-Perkins
Abundant Life Church
1717 Castle Drive
Garland, Texas 75040

Cover design by: David Butler
Layout and formatting by: Glynn M. Davis

ISBN 0-7414-3502-0

Published by:

INFINITY
PUBLISHING.COM

1094 New DeHaven Street, Suite 100
West Conshohocken, PA 19428-2713
Info@buybooksontheweb.com
www.buybooksontheweb.com
Toll-free (877) BUY BOOK
Local Phone (610) 941-9999
Fax (610) 941-9959

Printed in the United States of America

Printed on Recycled Paper

Published August 2006

Dedications

I want to thank our Lord and Savior for allowing me the privilege of writing this book. He blessed me as I read and typed the words He gave me. As you read the book, I pray the message touches your life, too. May the Lord of Heaven and Earth draw your heart closer to Him each day with HIS Great Love.

This book is dedicated to the following five Ministers and their wives. The Lord revealed to me; they are five of the pillars of my Spiritual House. They taught me to seek the truth in God's Word, which enabled me in my "life struggles" to find my way back to the Master Potter.

> Rev. Daniel & Patsy Stratton, Dallas, TX
>
> Rev. Charles & Gail Warman, Blytheville, AR
>
> Rev. & Mrs. Mark Hamby, Ft.Worth, TX
>
> Dr. Ernest Merrell & Dr. Ruby Merrell, Orange, CA
>
> Pastors Glynn & Carolyn Davis, Garland, TX

And my Special Thanks to: Pastors Glynn & Carolyn Davis, because they believe in the Almighty God who restores broken vessels, and equips them for His service.

In HIS service,

Betty McFall-Perkins

Acknowledgements

First of all, I would like to acknowledge Madora Hilton who said, "Go type this because you will lose it, if you don't."

Second, I want to express my appreciation to Greg Whaley for his long hours of proof reading, over and over and over. And his wonderful editing abilities.

And third, I want to thank all the people that proofed this little book and found my typo's, misused words and punctuation: Alice Millen, Terri Hilton, Peggy Jones, Marie Daniel and Christine Timm.

And as a special recognition: I want to thank my young grand daughter for her heart felt attempts to draw a book cover for me. Nataly Jo Perkins, at age nine diligently worked all day drawing picture after picture. Giving up, thinking she had not accomplished the assignment.

One Saturday morning, after I had actually paid for someone to draw the cover. I looked at my grand daughter's drawings, scattered on the table in disarray, I got out the professional copy along side Nataly's, and knew without a doubt she had captured the heart of the book. All we needed to do was add color.

I would like to mention all the people that read this little book and would not put it down until they finished reading it, because this encouraged me to get the book published. And all the people that said, "I want one when you get it published."

Acknowledgements

And my niece, Debra Bolin, who beat me to heaven, while the book was a work in progress. She was a perfect little pot that God did work miracles in, in the midst of her suffering, He revealed His Glory. Debbie loved the story.

I will be forever grateful for Pastor Glynn Davis who has put forth the much-needed effort to get the layout and "just right" finishing touches on the book, completed. And for helping bring a childhood dream to pass.

Thank all of you, for being one of The Master's devoted servants. And if you feel you are to small, just wait, you are in HIS hands, also. The Master is faithful to grow us up for His plans and purposes for our lives. God bless you.

In HIS service,
Betty McFall-Perkins

ABOUT THE AUTHOR

Betty McFall-Perkins, born Feb. 20, 1949 to Samuel Taylor McFall and Jessie Lee Olive McFall. I have been a firm believer in the Lord Jesus Christ since I was three years old. I was a little clay vessel and I had to find my way to the Master Potter.

I started my life believing in Jesus Christ, however, I wanted to fit in with the world. I would switch back and forth over my lifetime to cope with my selfish, demanding emotions. Until I had dug a pit and pulled the dirt in over my head, and then I cried out to the only One that could help me. And the Lord was faithful. He remembered the little girl that had said in her heart at age 7, "I want to be like my Father". Little did I know the father I wanted was the Lord God Almighty, my heavenly Father.

Table of Contents

1	The Promise	1
2	Great Expectations	5
3	Top Of The Heap	7
4	Heaven	11
5	The Land Of Depression	15
6	Surrender	19
7	The Tight Grip Of Fear	21
8	The Shepherdess	23
9	Broken Pieces	25
10	Trials Of Life	29
11	The Path To The Master Potter's House	33
12	The New Promise	35

1
The Promise

The Master Potter was working at His potter's wheel early in the morning, while the air was cool. He had made numerous beautiful vessels of clay. Many were tall and slender; some were round and had plenty of room inside. Others were just plain little pots. "Perfect," said the Master. The Master Potter had special plans for each one. All the vessels had a job to do and the Master was to send them out into the world on a mission.

The Master Potter worked at a steady pace getting His pots ready and sorted each according to His special assignment. There was something going on and each vessel knew they were involved. The excitement grew that morning with every passing minute. The vessels were expecting great things and they knew the Master Potter had perfect skills. He had given each one of them specific talents that would help them complete their assignments.

A Heap Of Broken Vessels

As the Potter worked, He noticed a small portion of clay He had left over from the early morning. "Now," He said, "The air is still cool enough and I have some time to work. I'll make a small pot. This one won't be as large as the other pots, but it will do for certain occasions. A smaller pot will keep the larger vessels from being used when they could be holding water from the well or storing grain." The Potter worked longer on the detail of the small pot. To give the Little Pot an added attraction He put a pretty curved handle on the side. The Little Pot stood out from all the other pots and vessels. This pot was precious to the Master Potter because He had special plans in the future for this particular pot.

However, the Little Pot stirred within himself and asked " Now, why am I so different from the rest of the pots? I am short and I can't see as well as my brothers and sisters. I am different in color and I am marked because my handle is different, too. Everybody will be staring at me, watching me, expecting me to be perfect. After all, I'm only a clay pot. What can I do that will make a big difference?" The Little Pot became very self-conscious of his handle. Sometimes the handle got in the way, so, the Little Pot decided to talk to the Master Potter and voice his concerns. Not a minute too soon either, because the Master was about to put the Little Pot in the furnace and bake him to make him strong.

"Um, um, A-um, Master Potter, I..., I..., I...I, ah, would like to ask you, Sir, why did you make me so small and insignificant? Why can't I be like the other pots? I would really like to be used on the altar; perhaps while I am still damp and plyable you could make me larger. Then I could hold the tears of the saints in heaven. I could hold the prayers of the saints, I could hold the wine You made from water, I could hold the meal in the widow's house. Oh, Master Potter," said the Little Pot longingly. "Couldn't you make me taller and round me out so I would fit into the scheme of things a little better? You know, I would like to be something special !" blurted out the troubled Little Pot.

"Have faith, Little Pot," is all the Potter would say. Then the Master Potter voiced a notable sigh and said, " I am the Master Potter. You are the clay; I have made you for my glory, not yours. If you will put your trust in ME, I will make your way straight and I will stay with you always." The Little Pot had a tear in his eye and said under his breath, "Well, perhaps tomorrow the Master will change his mind. He didn't exactly say No."

A Heap Of Broken Vessels

2
Great Expectations

The Little Pot went to his sisters and brothers and began to brag, "I am going to accomplish great things. I will be traveling and I will see the whole world. I had a talk with the Master Potter and I told him I wanted to be special." Totally confident was the Little Pot that the Master had spent more time on him and had given him the special little handle. "What if my handle does get in the way sometimes? I may be small, but I've got some really good ideas running around inside these clay walls," muttered the grumpy Little Pot.

The other pots and vessels weren't sure the Little Pot knew what he was talking about. The larger vessels knew they were going to be used and sent by the Master to do their jobs. They also knew He wouldn't waste His time on them if He didn't have a plan. So they laughed at the Little Pot and tried to warn him, "You better watch all these great expectations. You are setting yourself up for disappointment. Pride goes before destruction and an haughty spirit before a fall." One of the kinder vessels said to the Little Pot, " Wait on the Master. He will give you an assignment. Have faith in the Master."

The Little Pot shrugged his shoulders and spun around with a little grin and said, "You're just jealous, that's all. The Master and I had a talk just like I told you. He will do all that I asked, wait and see! The Master made me special." The Little Pot shuddered at the very thought of it not being true. No, he couldn't tolerate the thought.

3
Top Of The Heap

As the years passed, the Little Pot grew weary from waiting on the revelation of his job. "Exactly what is my job? What is the reason for my being formed and fashioned the way I am? Can't the Master spare a minute to talk to me? Time is passing me by. I think I will just get busy and see what I'm missing. I will find myself a place. I can do it all by myself!" pouted the Little Pot.

The Little Pot went wandering around looking for his place and found a home. It was a giant altar right in front of everyone. He was in full sight of all the people. "All right, this is perfect. Someone will notice me for sure; I am right up front. Any second now somebody will stop and admire my special gifts," daydreamed the Little Pot. The Little Pot sat there for a very long time, hoping that he would be noticed. After all, the Master Potter had taken a keen interest in shaping him and making him special.

A Heap Of Broken Vessels

Finally, one day, one of the keepers of the altar started removing all the pots. The clay pots were outdated and some had cracks and chips. The old pots were being replaced right in front of his eyes with bright, shining, gold pots. The gold pots all matched and had a nice handle on each side.

"What an insult!" burst out the indignant Little Pot, "Now why didn't I get two handles? Why is someone else taking my place? I was here first! I am the one that looked and sought out my place on the altar. After all, didn't I tell the Master I wanted to work on the altar?" About this time, the young altar worker picked up the dazed and startled Little Pot and tossed him right on top of the heap of broken vessels.

The Little Pot had a tight feeling run through his potbelly and it hurt something fierce. The pain was excruciating. He felt so humiliated that he had been tossed away by the very ones he had chosen to serve. As the pain ran its course and the Little Pot regained his self control, he gathered all the courage he could muster and jumped from the pile of broken and cracked pots. He ran as fast as he could but, he couldn't run fast enough to get away from his broken heart. "One good thing, I'm still in good shape. There isn't a crack not a sign of one. I don't have any chips at all. I have taken a close examination of myself; I don't see anything wrong with me," sniffed the Little Pot. "Besides, who cares anyway? Nobody ever noticed me. Maybe they will miss me now that I'm gone." He didn't pay any attention to the bitterness creeping into his clay. Anger toward the Master Potter was seeping deep inside.

As time went on the Little Pot didn't seem to care or remember anything about "that old altar". Time kept passing and the Little Pot just sat and stewed over his mistreatment and failings. Not once did he call on the Master to help him. He had completely forgotten the promise of the Master Potter.

A Heap Of Broken Vessels

4
Heaven

"**M**y dreams are coming true. My dreams are coming true," sang the Little Pot. "I found one of my brothers and he says there might just be a place for me at the altar in heaven. HEAVEN! Can you imagine me in Heaven? ME? Me, serving the heavenly host! OH! What a wonderful, wonderful thing to happen to me."

"See, I told you the Potter listened to me. I know it was years ago but the Master Potter is still watching over me. I think I remember Him telling me He would never leave me. Oh, I am so happy! I can go work at the altar in heaven! It must be the most beautiful, lavish place in all eternity! ME? An interview with Gabriel or with God! So I finally made it. I have found my place after all. The hardships have been worth it.

I finally found a place for me," chimed the Little Pot.

Upon his arrival in heaven, the Little Pot was ushered into a waiting- room. A very nice Angel that seemed to float approached the Little Pot. "Little Pot," spoke the Angel as he fluttered his wings softly, "You will need to wait until the time for an interview can be scheduled. Someone will be with you as soon as possible." Then the Angel wrote something in a book and flew off to meet another new arrival.

There appeared another Angel right before the Little Pot's eyes. Angels seemed to be everywhere and they all had that need to flutter their wings. " I must remember to ask why they do this fluttering," sighed the Little Pot. "O, that is to help us float in the air," replied the Angel, "and we do have an appointment arranged for you. The Head Angel will be with you shortly." The second Angel disappeared with another new arrival.

"They sure do move quickly up here. I wonder if I can keep up with them?" questioned the Little Pot under his breath. "You'll do fine, just fine," responded another Angel passing the Little Pot. "They must have super good hearing up here" sighed the Little Pot. "Everything is pure here in heaven. Even our thoughts are heard by God," responded the Angel to the Little Pot. And the Angel flew off once again.

The Little Pot waited and waited. It seemed all eternity would pass before the time for his appointment. Then he had to wait longer. He waited so long that he eventually forgot the interview and fell into a deep sleep.

The Little Pot started dreaming of his fabulous future, working with the Angels. He was abruptly awakened with a sound so loud that it shook the very walls of his being. Too scared and frightened to move, he waited to find out what was going on. An Angel, so tall he could hardly see the halo above his head, was staring down at the Little Pot.

The Angel whisked him off his little nesting place and escorted him outside the Pearly Gates. The Angel gently told the Little Pot, "First of all, you are too small and you still have some growing to do. Second, you really do have to die before you can come to heaven. Third, you fell asleep and missed the interview with the Head Angel of the altar. Tisk! Tisk! No wonder Gabriel blew his horn so near your ear. You needed a wake up call."

The angel spread his wings, bent over and whispered to the Little Pot in confidence, "It will be alright, Little Pot, because, we know all things work together for good to them that love God, to them who are the called according to HIS purpose."

5
The Land Of Depression

Crushed to the very core of his clay, the Little Pot was so devastated he couldn't find a tear left. "I waited for so many years and now what? What will I ever do? My brothers and sisters are gone off to service and here I am, scared and alone. Oh, how awful it is to be alone. I can't make it by myself," confessed the Little Pot, with a cry for help in his voice.

Standing there feeling lost, scared and abandoned the Little Pot made his way forward on a path that seemed endless. Nobody noticed or seemed to care which way he went. Not one soul stopped to inquire of his feelings or offer any compassion. They were much too busy scurrying around to do as their masters bid them.

The path got harder to see and the way was long and dim. It was getting harder to see by the minute as a dark, damp fog settled over the Little Pot.

It was depression, the very essence of depression. The depression spread over the Little Pot and it would be years before he could break out of the fog.

The unfamiliar Land of Depression was dark indeed. There was very little light in this area. The Little Pot could not find his way. The Little Pot just roamed around until he was exhausted and fell asleep. The nightmares were the worst. Some of the nightmares lasted all night. His dreams were brokenhearted, dreary and filled with the pain of rejection every night. Always, the Little Pot woke up more tired than when he went to sleep. It was a struggle to get up every morning.

Slowly the dreams started to change. The Little Pot started dreaming that he was looking for a new house, not just any house but a home. He wanted to belong, and to be a part of something or someone. "Surely there has to be a way out of the cold, dark dampness of depression and into the warm light of day," thought the Little Pot.

"You are special, you are special. I will never leave you and if you follow me, I will lead you on the Pathway of Life. You have work to do for ME." The haunting thought was like a wee, small voice from deep inside.

The voice beckoned the Little Pot onward and reassured him; He did have a job to do! "Oh, No! I am not willing to give up! Isn't it possible for something good to come out of all my experiences? Isn't that what the angel said so many years ago? Maybe, if I keep going forward and put the past behind me, I can be useful doing something. Anything, anything at all is better than nothing," shouted the Little Pot. "I know I have value!"

"The Potter made me for his glory. He told me so!" exclaimed the Little Pot. The Little Pot began to leap and shout as he danced about, celebrating with all his might. In fact, he was leaping and shouting so loud, the cloud of depression burst. The sunshine poured into the land and filled it with a beautiful rainbow of promise. The Little Pot couldn't remember seeing or feeling anything this spectacular in years.

A Heap Of Broken Vessells

6
Surrender

Once more the Little Pot started seeking to find his dreams. He kept marching valiantly ahead. Not looking to the left or to the right. He had his mind made up that he would succeed no matter what the cost. The world was a big place for such a Little Pot. He felt sure he could find a new town and make some friends. He didn't have any real friends. After all, maybe, a friend was the answer.

The Little Pot didn't have a minute to question his thoughts when he saw a Roman soldier approaching. The soldier was down-to-his-sandals tired and needed a drink of water. The man marched toward the Little Pot in a deadly silence that comes over one in deep thought. He was constantly planning and working out strategy for victory over his opponents, wondering how to bring about an attack in total surprise. These thoughts consumed the man and you could read them on his face. The look on the soldier's face scared the Little Pot.

Nevertheless, his loneliness overcame his fear

and the Little Pot surrendered to the soldier so that he could get a drink of water. The soldier was in such a hurry that he didn't notice the unusual quality of the Little Pot. He surely didn't want to take the Little Pot with him. After he had quickly gulped his fill, the man walked off abruptly and left the Little Pot sitting there alone.

Whew!" gasped the Little Pot as he wiped the sweat off his brow. "That was a close call! I am so glad he didn't take me to war with him. I have heard all about these Roman soldiers and their ruthless, bloody battles," admitted the Little Pot, still stunned by the hardness of the soldier.

7
The Tight Grasp Of Fear

Early the next morning before the sun had a chance to color the sky and the stars were still faintly twinkling; the sound of thunder boomed loud and clear. Suddenly, without warning, the ledge of the well where the Little Pot was sitting was quickly surrounded by shepherds and their animals. They were running, pushing and calling out to one another. The ground shook from the weight of the sheep and camels.

The Little Pot was shaking, too. At any moment the Little Pot felt he might be knocked off the wall and into the well. Before he could get that thought out of his head, before he could feel the tight grip of fear engulf him, there he went! Bottom over top, top over bottom, round and round, down, down into the depths of the well.

With a sobering splash he landed in the water. Cold, balmy waves of water were all around him. "I am not sinking yet, but any minute I know I am going to the most dangerous place I have ever been in all my years; the bottom of the well! I don't know what could be at the bottom of this well! I do know I am about to find out! I'm in too deep," chattered the cold, scared Little Pot. The stark reality saturated his clay walls as the cold, gentle waves tossed him this way and that way in a rocking motion.

His concern about the water was quickly dismissed as he caught a glimpse of a very large clay pot above him. The Little Pot realized even greater harm was about to befall him. A clay pot big enough to smash this little clay pot to pieces, if he didn't move fast. Just as the big, clay pot was about to land on top of him; a wonderful wave pushed the Little Pot aside. What a tremendous relief flooded through him!

The waves grew stronger and stronger as he was tossed to and fro with each dip of the big, clay pot. All at once, a very strong wave pushed him into the big water pot. As fast as he had met with disaster, he felt new hope rise inside himself. The Little Pot began to feel the ascent to the top of the well and he knew this was an unusual ending to a bad event.

8

The Shepherdess

Light! Glorious light, shining into the little pot. He was blinded by the brightness of the light and blinked hard to get his sight back. The Little Pot was rubbing his eyes when he felt warm, gentle hands about him and they were hugging him close.

"Look! Look what I found," exclaimed Chloe. "It was in the water pot. How long do you think it was in the well? It appears old and worn. See, it has it's own handle and it is perfectly made. Who could have lost such a treasure? Who could lose such a wonderful cup?" questioned the young shepherdess.

Her friends didn't seem as interested as young Chloe. In fact, they didn't seem to share Chloe's delight at all. For the time being, Chloe tucked the little cup into her shepherd's bag to keep it safe.

"Cup? Cup? What did she say? Cup! Why, I am a little pot. The Master Potter would have told me if I were a CUP. Surely there is some mistake. A CUP! I... , I..., I..., can't be a cup, what can a cup do? For certain it can't hold enough grain for a pantry. I know a cup isn't as important as a POT that God can work a miracle in! That is what I want to be!" yelled the red-faced Little Pot in total disbelief.

9
Broken Pieces

Chloe finished watering her sheep and turned her thoughts toward the meadow in the valley. This day Chloe had new purpose in her step. She knew exactly where to take her sheep and the Little Cup. She was headed for the valley where sweet, green grasses grow in a wonderful meadow.

This valley has a stream that flows from high in the mountains with crystal clear water. The water rushes downstream and sends little cascades of bubbles over the rocks. It flows jubilantly down the middle of the meadow into an underground spring at the end of the valley.

Only this morning, Chloe was headed to the foothills of the valley. Straight to the rock house where the old man lives. He was the Master Potter and He dug His clay from the hills around the base of the mountains. The Potter would know to whom the Little Cup belonged. He would know by the clay.

Chloe put her mind on the sheep and busied herself with the job at hand. She marched along with the sheep and started singing a happy song to them as she led them to the green pasture. While she was singing, she heard a new voice join in with hers.

Chloe turned to see the Old Man walking beside her. The unexpected sight of the Potter gave her a feeling of happiness she couldn't explain.

Her story of the Little Cup came to life very quickly. The young sheepherder was so excited her words were tripping and falling all over each other, as she tried to tell the Master Potter how she found the Little Cup. "Take a deep breath, Chloe," instructed the Potter. "Now, try it again, slow and calmly."

"I found this Little Cup. Look! Let me show you! It is right here," motioned Chloe as she groped in her shepherd's bag. Chloe pulled the Little Cup out of the bag and started to unwrap it. "Do you know this cup? Do you know to whom it might belong? It was in the well and it came up inside of the water pot, as I drew water for the sheep. You know it has wonderful colors in it and it must belong to someone. Who could lose such a great Little Cup?"

Much to Chloe's dismay, the Little Cup had lost

his handle. The broken and cracked pieces were lying in her trembling hands as she finished unwrapping the Little Cup. She burst into tears and with her chin quivering, she turned to the Master Potter.

Gently and tenderly the Master Potter said, "Yes, I know this Little Cup. I made this Little Cup myself many years ago. Now, now, don't waste your tears. I can repair all the damage to this Little Cup. Let me take him with me and I will return him once he is strong and ready to work again," consoled the Master Potter. "You tend to your father's sheep and I will tend to the little clay cup." Chloe gazed deep into the Potter's eyes and she knew He would keep His promise.

A Heap Of Broken Vessels

10
Trials Of Life

The Master Potter turned His full attention to the Little Cup. He saw a few pits and some thin, hairline cracks were starting to form. "Master, Master Potter, I am so glad to see you. Will you help me? I have been so alone and afraid," cried the Little Cup.

The Little Cup poured out his heart to the Potter. The Potter listened closely to the Little Cup, nodding His head as he finished his account. The Master Potter said, "Yes, yes, you have been on a long journey through the Trials of Life. You are in a learning process right now. First, you need to grow in your spirit. Second, you need to learn to depend on me. Learn to do my will instead of your own," comforted the Master. "You and I need to take a look at these cracks and pits. For instance, observe these cracks. Notice the way the cracks run; they start with doubt and travel with unbelief. Bitterness starts to spring up when you

A Heap Of Broken Vessels

don't forgive and bitterness has roots. Once bitterness gets into the cracks, it spreads. Bitterness opens the door to many dangerous enemies of the Spirit. Forgiveness is the greatest weapon against bitterness," explained the Master Potter.

" These pits of oppression must go, too. When distress tries to overpower you, robe yourself in the Garments of Praise for the Spirit of Heaviness. The sacrifice of praise will lift you to new heights. It works every time when you praise the Lord with all your heart," concluded the Potter.

" I will fill your pits and cracks with an armor of love that will guard your heart. I must put you back in the oven and bake you to make you strong. You will be established and you will do a work for me," promised the Master Potter.

The Master Potter worked diligently on the golden armor of love. "There is no fear in love; perfect love cast out fear: because fear has torment. He that fears is not made perfect in love," offered the Master. "I want you to be perfected. A little longer in the oven perhaps, then on with the Trials of Life. This will make a great difference in your character. Learn to build good character. Use your freedom of choice wisely," advised the Potter.

"Little Cup you are very small and exquisite.

However, you must remember: It isn't your size or your uniqueness that creates value; it is what you put inside of your cup. You must be filled with love, peace and joy. You need to realize that a pot is used for storing and preserving its' contents.

A cup is for overflowing and pouring out. A cup is what I created and a cup is what I need you to be. You need to develop a Servant's Heart," enlightened the Master Potter. The surprised Little Cup was filled with anticipation.

11
Path To The Master Potters House

For several days, the young girl kept the sheep grazing in all their favorite places. She climbed the remote path of the shepherds: always looking for new pastures and good foliage for the sheep. After a week, Chloe finally led the sheep back over the familiar path to the cut-off that leads to the meadow below.

Chloe looked at the sky and saw it was a soft, brilliant, azure blue with big, white clouds majestically floating in the breeze. The weather would be great for a trip to the valley. She would walk slowly and not hurry, as the path turned and twisted all the way down.

The closer Chloe and her small flock got to the green pastures, the more she felt the excitement rise within her. The sheep seemed to notice Chloe was different today and felt the excitement, too.

The sheep were following close to Chloe. When the flock arrived at the meadow, the older ewes sniffed the air and looked for a place to eat. The little lambs were already nibbling the tender new shoots of green grass. The descent down the mountain had brought on hunger.

Chloe took a count to make sure all the sheep were safely down the side of the mountain. Then Chloe found her favorite spot under a very large oak tree. From there she could watch over the flock. Chloe placed her shepherd's bag under the big oak and burst into a song of praise that filled the valley and kept the sheep calm and quiet.

12
The New Promise

It was a perfect day and all was well with the young sheepherder. She walked among the sheep checking them and speaking softly as the morning flowed into midday. The air was getting warmer as the day gained momentum and the grass lost its dew. Soon it would be time to eat lunch.

The lunch of a sheepherder was very humble and Chloe was no different. She reached into her shepherd's bag and pulled out the pieces of cheese and bread to bless. She began to eat and think how nice it would be to have the Little Cup to get a drink from the stream.

Chloe was walking toward the stream when she felt the Master Potter matching each of her steps. She looked up without surprise, to see Him smiling at her. His smile at once cheered her heart and washed away any anxiety she was feeling. A smile started to form at the corners of her mouth and she broke into pure laughter when she saw the Little

A Heap Of Broken Vessels

Cup. Tears filled her eyes and she brushed them away with the back of her hands and dried her face with the hem of her shawl. The Master Potter gave the cherished Little Cup to Chloe. Chloe turned toward the stream and dipped the cup into the water then lifted the cup towards the Potter and said, "Surely my cup runneth over with joy!"

The Master Potter spent the afternoon with Chloe. He told her all about the Little Cup's journey and all he had overcome. Then the Potter left her with her gift, returning to His work. Chloe watched the back of the Master Potter for as far as she could see Him in the distance. There was something mysterious about the Potter. He seemed to be there beside her sometimes when she least expected Him.

Chloe shook off her thoughts and turned to the sheep. Chloe wanted to lead the sheep to the higher pastures where the grass was greener and taller. She had often heard of this place and now she was ready to attempt the climb. Chloe felt stronger and braver than she had ever felt before. She was inspired to climb, climb higher.

The Little Cup was nestled safely in the warmth of Chole's shepherd's bag. He could rest to the sway and bounce of the lively pace of Chole. The sheep's gentle bleating sounds blended with the music of the outdoors, as Chloe lead the way to her Father's house.

The Little Cup's dream of belonging was coming true. As he relaxed and drifted towards sleepiness, his thought

The New Promise

turned to the Promise of the Master Potter. There were plans for his future and he was wondering just how he was going to get the servant's heart the Master told him about. The Little Cup fell asleep pondering about his new heart, his servant's heart, which is another story for another day.

Betty McFall-Perkins is availble to speak at Women's Meetings of any size. She shares an incredible testimony of the Grace of God that brought her complete restoration. Her faith in God will bring hope to those who feel like they have been discarded in a heap of broken vessels, as well as to the whole.

She has now found her life's calling and is in pursuit of her God given destiny. Betty can be contacted at:

       Betty Lou McFall-Perkins
       Abundant Life Church
       1717 Castle Drive
       Garland, Texas 75040

       Phone: 972-272-8838
       Email: Onetruegospel@aol.com